UNION &
COMMUNION

J. Hudson Taylor

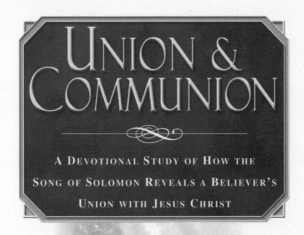

UNION &
COMMUNION

A DEVOTIONAL STUDY OF HOW THE
SONG OF SOLOMON REVEALS A BELIEVER'S
UNION WITH JESUS CHRIST

BETHANY HOUSE PUBLISHERS
MINNEAPOLIS, MINNESOTA 55438

Union and Communion
J. Hudson Taylor

Updated edition
Copyright © 2000
Bethany House Publishers

Published by Bethany House Publishers
A Ministry of Bethany Fellowship International
11400 Hampshire Avenue South
Minneapolis, Minnesota 55438
www.bethanyhouse.com

Printed in the United States of America by
Bethany Press International, Minneapolis, Minnesota 55438

Library of Congress Cataloging-in-Publication Data
Taylor, James Hudson, 1832–1905.
　　Union & communion / by J. Hudson Taylor.
　　　　p. cm.
Rev. ed. of: Union and communion with Christ. 1993.
　　ISBN 0-7642-2352-6
　　1. Bible. O.T. Song of Solomon—Commentaries. I. Title: Union
and communion. II. Taylor, James Hudson, 1832–1905. Union and
communion with Christ. III. Title.
　　BS1485.3.T39　2000
223′.907—dc21　　　　　　　　　　　　　　　　　99–050974

Foreword

*T*his book, the design of which is to lead the serious Bible student into the green pastures of the Good Shepherd, then to the banqueting house of the King, and finally to the service of the vineyard, is one of the abiding legacies of J. Hudson Taylor to the church. In the power of an obvious unction from the Holy One, he has been enabled to unfold in simplest language the deep truth of the believer's personal union with the Lord, which under symbol and imagery is the subject of the Song of Songs. And in so doing, he has ministered unfailing guidance to one of the most commonly neglected and misunderstood books of the sacred Scriptures. How many have said of the richness of the language and depth of the imagery that both conceal and reveal the book's meaning, "How can I understand except someone guide me?" It is safe to say that these pages cannot fail to help and to bless all such students of the Word.

To those who knew him, Hudson Taylor's life emphasized the value of this small volume. For what he here expounds he also lived out in his everyday life. If his words indicate the possibility and blessedness of union with Christ, his whole life declared it in actual experience. He lived as one who was "married to another, even to Him who is raised from the dead," and the outcome of that union was fruit brought forth unto God. What he *was* has given meaning and confirmation to what he has *written*. This cannot be exaggerated. It is inevitable that there are those who will read and reject as mystical and impractical that which is so directly concerned with the intimacies of fellowship with the unseen Lord. I would, however, venture to remind such that the writer of these pages founded the China Inland Mission. He translated his vision of the Beloved into lifelong service, and so kept it undimmed through the years of a life hardly paralleled in our day.

The commendation of the following chapters proclaim a message distilled from experience and form at least a track through this fenced portion of God's Word that will lead many who tread it into the joys of Emmanuel's land.

J. J. Stuart Holden

Contents

Introduction 9

About the Title 15

1. The Unsatisfied Life and Its Remedy 17

2. Communion Broken . . . and Restored 35

3. The Joy of Unbroken Communion 47

4. Communion Broken Again . . . and Restored 57

5. The Fruits of a Recognized Union 69

6. Unrestrained Communion 81

Appendix: The Daughters of Jerusalem 93

Introduction

*T*he great purpose toward which all the dispensational dealings of God tend is revealed to us in 1 Corinthians 15:28: "That God may be all in all." In agreement with this is the teaching of our Lord in John 17:3: "And this is [the object of] eternal life: that they may know you, the only true God, and Jesus Christ whom you have sent." This being so, should we not act wisely by keeping this object ever before us in our daily life and study of God's holy Word?

All Scripture is given by inspiration of God and is profitable. Therefore, no part is or can be neglected without loss. Few portions of the Word will help the serious student more in the pursuit of this all-important knowledge of God than the much-neglected book, Song of Solomon. Like other portions of the Word of God, this book has its difficulties. But the fact that it surpasses our unaided powers of comprehension and research is an indication of its divine origin. Can finite humanity expect to grasp divine power or to understand and interpret the works or the providences of the All-Wise God? And if not, is it surprising that His Word needs supernatural wisdom to aid us in its interpretation? Thanks be to God, the illumination of the Holy Spirit is promised to all who seek it. What more could we desire?

This book, especially, is unintelligible without the key, but that key is easily found in the teachings of the New Testament. The Incarnate Word is the true key to the written Word; but even before the Incarnation, a student of the Old Testament would have found help to understand the mysteries of this book in the prophetic writings, for in them Israel was taught that her Maker was her husband. John the Baptist, the last of the prophets, recognized the Bridegroom in the person of Christ, and said, "He who has the bride is the bridegroom. The friend of the bridegroom, who stands and hears him, rejoices greatly at the bridegroom's voice. For this reason my joy has been fulfilled" (John 3:29). Paul goes still further, in the fifth chapter of Ephesians, and teaches that the union of Christ with His church, and her subjection to Him, underlies the marriage relationship and affords the pattern for every godly union.

In Solomon, the bridegroom king as well as the author of this poem, we have a type of our Lord, the true Prince of Peace, in His coming reign. At that time will be found not merely His bride, the church, but also a willing people, His subjects, over whom He shall reign gloriously. Distant potentates will bring their wealth and will behold the glory of the enthroned King, proving Him with hard questions, as did the Queen of Sheba to King Solomon, and blessed will be those to whom this privilege is accorded. A brief glance will suffice them for a lifetime, but what shall be the royal dignity and blessedness of the risen and exalted bride? Forever with her Lord, forever like her Lord, forever conscious that His desire is toward her, she will share alike His heart and His throne! Can a study of the book that helps us to understand these mysteries of grace and love be other than profitable?

It is interesting to notice the contrast between this book of the Bible and the one preceding it. The book of Ecclesiastes teaches that all is vanity, and thus is a fitting introduction to the Song of Solomon, which shows how true blessing and satisfaction are found. In like manner, our Savior's teaching in John 4 points out the powerlessness of earthly things to give lasting satisfaction, in striking contrast to the flow of blessing that results from the presence of the Holy Spirit—whose work it is to reveal Christ as the Bridegroom of the soul: "Everyone who drinks of this water will be thirsty again, but those who drink of the water that I will give them will never be thirsty. The water that I will give will become in them a spring of water gushing up [overflowing, on and on] to eternal life" (John 4:13–14).

I have found it helpful to divide the book into six sections, which make up the six chapters of this volume. In each section we will find the speakers to be the bride, the Bridegroom, and the daughters of Jerusalem. It is not usually difficult to ascertain the speaker, although with some of the verses scholars have arrived at different conclusions. The bride speaks of the Bridegroom as her "beloved"; the Bridegroom speaks of her as His "love," while the address of the daughters of Jerusalem is more varied. In the first five chapters, they style her as the fairest among women, but in the sixth she is spoken of as the Shulammite, or the King's bride, and also as the Prince's daughter.

I have found it helpful to mark my Bible to indicate the speakers. The bride is the chief speaker in sections 1 and 2, and is quite occupied with herself; but in section 3, where the communion is unbroken, she has little to say and appears as the listener; the daughters of Jerusalem give a long address, and the Bridegroom His longest. In this section, for the first time, He calls her His bride and woos her to fellowship in service. In section 4, the bride again is the chief speaker, but after her restoration the Bridegroom speaks at length. In section 5, we notice the bride is no longer called "the fairest among women" but claims herself to be and is recognized as the royal bride. In section 6, the Bridegroom claims her from her very birth and not merely from her espousal to Him, as God in Ezekiel 16 claimed Israel.

In the secret of His presence
How my soul delights to hide!
Oh, how precious are the lessons
Which I learn at Jesus' side!
Earthly cares can never vex me,
Neither trials lay me low;
For when Satan comes to vex me,
To the secret place I go!

About the Title

"The Song of Songs, which is Solomon's."

Well may this book be called *the* Song of Songs. There is no song like it. Read aright, it brings gladness to the heart that far exceeds the joy of earthly things even as heaven is higher than the earth. It has been well said that this is a song that grace alone can teach and experience alone can learn. Our Savior, speaking of the union of the branch with the vine, adds, "I have said these things to you so that my joy may be in you, and that your joy may be complete" (John 15:11). And the beloved disciple, writing of Him who was from the beginning, who was with the Father and was revealed to us in order that we might share in the fellowship that He enjoys, says that he writes these things so that our joy may be complete. Union with Christ and abiding in Christ—what do they secure? Peace, perfect peace; rest, constant rest; answers to all our prayers; victory over all our foes; pure, holy living; ever-increasing fruitfulness. All of these are the glad outcome of abiding in Christ. To deepen this union, to make more constant this abiding, is the practical use of this precious book of the Bible.

1

The Unsatisfied Life and Its Remedy

Song of Solomon 1:2–2:7

———

*T*here should be no difficulty in recognizing the bride as the speaker in verses 2–7 of chapter 1. The words are not those of one dead in trespasses and sins, to whom the Lord is as a root out of dry ground—without form or majesty. The speaker has had her eyes opened to behold His beauty and longs for a fuller enjoyment of His love.

> Let him kiss me with the kisses of his mouth!
> For your love [endearments, caresses] is better than
> wine. (1:2)

And this is as it should be for the bride of Christ; it marks a distinct stage in the development of the life of grace in the soul. This recorded experience gives, as it were, a divine warrant for the desire for perceptible man-

17

ifestations of His presence—heartfelt communications of His love. It was not always so with her. Once she was content in His absence—other friendships and other occupations sufficed her—but now it can never be so again. The world can never be to her what it once was. The betrothed bride has learned to love her Lord, and no other companionship can satisfy her like companionship with Him. His visits may be occasional and brief, but they are precious times of pure enjoyment. Their memory is cherished in the intervals and their repetition longed for. There is no real satisfaction in His absence, and yet He is not always with her: He comes and goes. When He comes her joy in Him is like heaven, and when He goes she is longing in vain for His presence. Like the ever-changing tide, her experience is a constant ebb and flow. It may even be that unrest is the rule, satisfaction the exception.

Is there no help for this? Must it always continue this way? Is it possible that He has created these unquenchable longings only to taunt her? It is strange indeed if this is the case. Yet are there not many of the Lord's people whose daily experience corresponds with hers? They don't know the rest or the joy of abiding in Christ, and they don't know how to attain it or why it isn't theirs. There are many who look back to the delightful hour of their conversion who are far from finding the rich inheritance in Christ they once enjoyed, and they are conscious that they have lost their first love. They might express their experience in the sad lament, "Where is the blessedness I knew when first I saw the Lord?"

Others, who may not have lost their first love, may be feeling that the occasional interruptions to communion are becoming more and more unbearable. His absence is an ever-increasing distress: "Oh, that I knew where I might find Him! Would that His love were strong and constant like mine and that He never withdrew the light of His countenance!"

Poor mistaken one! There is a love far stronger than yours waiting, longing for satisfaction. The Bridegroom is waiting for you all the time, and the conditions that debar His approach are all of your *own* making. Take the right place before Him, and He will be most ready, most glad, to satisfy your deepest longings, and to meet and supply your every need.

What would we think of a bride whose conceit and self-will prevented not only the consummation of her own joy but also his who has given her his heart? Though never at rest in his absence, she cannot trust him fully when he is with her, and she does not care to give up her own name, her own rights, her possessions, or her will to him who has become necessary for her happiness.

She would claim him fully without giving herself fully to him.

But this can never be, for while she retains her own name she can never claim his. She may not promise to love and honor if she will not also promise to obey, and until her love reaches that point of surrender, she must remain an unsatisfied lover—until then she cannot be a satisfied bride who finds rest in the home of her husband. While she retains her own will and the control of her own possessions, she must be content to live on her own resources, for she cannot claim his.

Could there be a sadder proof of the reality and the extent of the fall of man than the deep-seated distrust of our loving Lord and Master that makes us hesitate to give ourselves up entirely to Him for fear He might require something beyond our powers or call for something that we might find hard to give or to do? The real secret of an unsatisfied life often lies in an unsurrendered will.

And yet how foolish and wrong this is! Do we imagine that we are wiser than He or that our love for ourselves is more tender and strong than His or that we know ourselves better than He does? How our distrust must grieve and wound afresh the tender heart of the Man of Sorrows!

How would an earthly bridegroom feel if he discovered that his bride-elect was dreading to marry him, fearing that when he had the power he would render her life insupportable? Yet how many of the Lord's redeemed ones treat Him in this way! No wonder they are neither happy nor satisfied!

True love cannot be stationary. It must either decline or grow. Despite all the unworthy fears of our poor hearts, divine love is destined to conquer. The bride continues to exclaim,

> Your anointing oils are fragrant,
> your name is perfume poured out;
> therefore the maidens love you. (1:3)

There is no oil like the oil with which the high priest was anointed. Our Bridegroom is a priest as well as a king. The trembling bride cannot wholly dismiss her fears, but the unrest and the longing become unbearable and she determines to surrender all and, come what may, to follow Him fully. She will yield her very self to Him, heart and hand, influence and possessions. Nothing can be so unbearable as His absence! If He leads to another Moriah, or even to a Calvary, she will follow Him.

> Draw me after you, let us make haste. (1:4)

And what follows this commitment? A wonderfully glad surprise. No Moriah. No Calvary. On the contrary, fellowship with a king! When the heart submits, Jesus reigns. And when Jesus reigns, there is pure rest.

And where does He lead His bride?

> The king has brought me into his chambers. (1:4)

Not first to the banqueting house—that will come in due season—but first to be alone with him.

How perfect! Could we be satisfied to meet a beloved one only in public? No, we want to take him aside—to have him all to ourselves. So with our Master: He takes His now fully consecrated bride aside to taste and enjoy the sacred intimacies of His wondrous love. The Bridegroom of His church longs for communion with His people more than His people long for fellowship with Him, and often cries,

> Let me see your face,
> > let me hear your voice;
> for your voice is sweet,
> > and your face is lovely. (2:14)

Are we not all too apt to seek Him because of our need rather than for His joy and pleasure? This should not be the case. We do not admire selfish children who, thinking only of what they can get from their parents, are not mindful of the pleasure they may give or the help they may offer. But are we not in danger of forgetting that pleasing God means giving Him pleasure? Some of us look back to the time when the words "to please God" meant no more than not to sin against Him or to grieve Him. But would earthly parents be satisfied with the mere absence of disobedience in their children? Would a bridegroom be satisfied if his bride only sought him for the supply of her needs?

A word about a morning quiet time may not be out of place here. There is no time so profitably spent as the early hour given to Jesus alone. Do we give sufficient attention to this hour? If at all possible, it should be redeemed. Nothing can make up for it.

Another thought: When we bring our questions to God, do we sometimes either go on to offer some other petition or leave the place of prayer without waiting for a reply? Doesn't this show little expectation of an answer much less desire for one? Would we like to be treated in this way? Quiet waiting before God saves us from many mistakes and many sorrows.

We find the bride making the glad discovery of a king—her King—and not a cross, as she expected. This is the firstfruit of her consecration.

> We will exult and rejoice in you;
>> we will extol your love more than wine;
>> rightly do they love you. (1:4b)

Another discovery no less important awaits her. She has seen the face of the King, and as the rising sun reveals what was hidden in the darkness, so His light has revealed her own blackness to her. "Ah," she cries, "I am black..." "...and beautiful," interjects the Bridegroom with inimitable grace and tenderness. "No, like the tents of Kedar," she continues. "Yet to Me," He responds, "you are lovely like the curtains of Solomon!" (See 1:5.)

Nothing humbles the soul like sacred and intimate communion with the Lord; yet there is a sweet joy in feeling that *He* knows *all* and loves us still. Things once called small oversights are now seen with new eyes in the secret of His presence. And here we see the mistake, the sin of not keeping our own vineyard. This the bride confesses:

> Do not gaze at me because I am dark,
>   because the sun has gazed on me.
> My mother's sons were angry with me;
>   they made me keeper of the vineyards,
>   but my own vineyard I have not kept! (1:6)

Our attention is here drawn to a danger that is real in our day: The intense activity of our lives may lead to zeal in service to the neglect of personal communion. Such neglect will not only lessen the value of the service but will also tend to incapacitate us for the highest service. If we are watchful over the souls of others and neglectful of our own—if we are seeking to remove motes from our brother's eye, unmindful of the beam in our own, we shall often be disappointed with our powerlessness to help our brethren, while our Master will not be less disappointed in us. Let us never forget that what we are is more important than what we do and that all fruit borne while not abiding in Christ will be fruit of the flesh and not of the Spirit. As wounds when healed often leave a scar, so the sin of neglected communion may be forgiven and yet the effect remain permanently.

We now come to a very sweet evidence of the reality of the heart-union of the bride with her Lord. She is one with the Good Shepherd: Her heart goes intuitively forth to the feeding of the flock, but she would tread in the footsteps of Him whom her soul loves and would neither labor alone nor seek other companionship:

> Tell me, you whom my soul loves,
>   where you pasture your flock,
>   where you make it lie down at noon;
> for why should I be like one who is veiled
>   beside the flocks of your companions? (1:7)

She will not mistake the fellowship of His servants for that of their Master.

If you do not know,
　　O fairest among women,
follow the tracks of the flock,
　　and pasture your kids
　　beside the shepherds' tents. (1:8)

These are the words of the daughters of Jerusalem, and they give a correct reply to her questions. Let her show her love to her Lord by feeding His sheep, by caring for His lambs (see John 21:15–17), and she need not fear missing His presence. While sharing with other undershepherds in caring for His flock, she will find the Chief Shepherd at her side and enjoy the tokens of His approval. It will be service *with* Jesus as well as *for* Him.

But far sweeter than the reply of the daughters of Jerusalem is the voice of the Bridegroom, who now speaks himself. It is the living fruit of her heart-oneness with Him that makes His love break forth in the joyful refrain of verses 9–11. For it is not only true that our love for our Lord will show itself in feeding His sheep but also that He who said, "Inasmuch as you have done it unto one of the least of these my brethren, you have done it unto me," has His own heart-love stirred, and not infrequently reveals himself in a special way to those who are ministering for Him.

The commendation of the bride in verse 9 is one of striking appropriateness and beauty:

I compare you, my love,
to a mare among Pharaoh's chariots.

Horses originally came out of Egypt, and the pure breed still found in Arabia was brought during Solomon's reign by his merchants for all the kings of the East. Those selected for Pharaoh's own chariot would not only be of the purest blood and perfect in proportion and symmetry but also perfect in training, docile, and obedient; they would know no will but that of the charioteer, and the only object of their existence would be to carry the king wherever he wanted to go. So should it be with the church of Christ: one body with many members, indwelt and guided by one Spirit; holding the Head, and knowing no will but His. Her quick and harmonious movement should cause His kingdom to expand throughout the world.

Many years ago a beloved friend, returning from the East by the overland route, made the journey from the Suez to Cairo in the cumbersome stagecoach of the day. After the passengers took their places, a dozen wild young horses were harnessed to the vehicle with ropes. The driver took his seat, cracked his whip, and the horses dashed off, some to the right, some to the left, and others forward, causing the coach to start with a jerk and as suddenly to stop, the effect being first to throw those sitting in the front seat into the laps of those sitting behind, and then the reverse. With the aid of several Arabs running on each side to keep these wild animals moving in the right direction, the passengers were tossed and jolted, bruised and shaken, until, upon reaching their destination, they were too weary and sore to get the rest they so much needed.

Is not the church of God today more like these untrained steeds than a company of horses attached to Pharaoh's chariot? And while self-will and disunion are apparent in the church, can we wonder that the world still lies in the lap of the Wicked One and that the great heathen nations are barely touched?

Changing His simile, the Bridegroom continues:

Your cheeks are comely with ornaments,
    your neck with strings of jewels.
We will make you ornaments of gold,
    studded with silver. (1:10–11)

The bride is not only beautiful and useful to her Lord but she is also adorned, and it is His delight to add to her adornments. Nor are His gifts perishable flowers or trinkets destitute of intrinsic value: The finest of gold, the purest of silver, and the most precious and lasting of jewels are the gifts of the royal Bridegroom to His bride; and these, braided into her hair, increase the pleasure of the

One who has bestowed them.

In verse 12, the bride responds,

> While the king was on his couch,
>   my nard gave forth its fragrance.

It is in His presence and through His grace that whatever fragrance or beauty may be found in us comes forth. Of Him as its source, through Him as its instrument, and to Him as its end, is all that is gracious and divine. But *He* is better far than all that His grace works in us.

> My beloved is to me a bag of myrrh
>   that lies between my breasts.
> My beloved is to me a cluster of henna blossoms
>   in the vineyards of En-gedi. (1:13–14)

All is well when our eyes are filled with His beauty and our hearts are occupied with Him. In the measure in which this is true of us we will recognize the correlative truth that His great heart is occupied with us. Note the response of the Bridegroom:

> Ah, you are beautiful, my love;
>   ah, you are beautiful;
>   your eyes are doves. (1:15)

How can the Bridegroom truthfully use such words of one who recognizes herself as "black . . . like the tents of Kedar"? And still stronger are the Bridegroom's words in 4:7:

> You are altogether beautiful, my love;
>> there is no flaw in you.

We find the solution in 2 Corinthians 3:18. Moses, in contemplation of the divine glory, became so transformed that the Israelites were not able to look on the glory of his countenance. "And all of us, with unveiled faces, seeing [beholding] the glory of the Lord as though reflected in a mirror, are being transformed into the same image from one degree of glory to another [the brightness caught from His glory transforms us to glory]; for this comes from the Lord, the Spirit." Every mirror has two surfaces. The one is dull and unreflecting, spotted and blemished; but when the reflecting surface is turned fully toward us, we see no flaw; we see our own image. So while the bride is delighting in the beauty of the Bridegroom, He beholds His own image in her. There is no flaw in that image; it is all fair. May we ever present this reflection to His gaze and to the world in which we live, for His glory.

Note again His words:

> Your eyes are doves. (1:15)
> [or, you have dove's eyes.]

The hawk is a beautiful bird, and has beautiful eyes, quick and penetrating; but the Bridegroom does not desire a hawk's eyes in His bride. The tender eyes of the innocent dove are what He admires. It was as a dove that the Holy Spirit came upon Him at His baptism, and dove-like character is what He seeks for each of His people.

The reason why David was not permitted to build the temple was a very significant one. His life was far from perfect (his mistakes and sins have been faithfully recorded by the Holy Spirit). And though his sins brought upon him God's chastening, it was not any of these that disqualified him from building the temple; rather, it was his warlike spirit. Though many of his battles, if not all, were for the establishment of God's kingdom and the fulfillment of His promises to Abraham, Isaac, and Jacob, Solomon alone, the prince of peace, could build the temple. If we would be soul-winners and build up the church, which is His temple, let us remember, not by discussion nor by argument but by lifting up Christ will we draw men unto Him.

He has called her beautiful; wisely and well does she reply,

Ah, you are beautiful, my beloved,
   truly lovely.
Our couch is green;

the beams of our house are cedar,
our rafters are pine.
I am a rose of Sharon,
a lily of the valleys. (1:16–17; 2:1)

The last words are often quoted as though they were
the utterance of the Bridegroom, but I believe this to be
in error. The bride says in effect, "You call me fair and
pleasant, but the fairness and pleasantness are Yours; I
am but a wild flower, a lowly, scentless rose of Sharon
(i.e., the autumn crocus) or lily of the valley."

To this the Bridegroom responds, "Be it so; but if a
wild flower, yet . . ."

As a lily among brambles,
so is my love among maidens. (2:2)

Again the bride replies,

As an apple tree [the citron] among the trees of the
wood,
so is my beloved among young men.
With great delight I sat in his shadow,
and his fruit was sweet to my taste. (2:3)

The citron is a beautiful evergreen, affording delightful shade as well as refreshing fruit. A humble wild
flower herself, she recognizes her Bridegroom as a noble
tree, both ornamental and fruitful. Shade from the burn-

ing sun, refreshment and rest she finds in Him. What a contrast is her present position and feelings to those with which we began this section! He knew full well the cause of all her fears. Her distrust sprang from her ignorance of Him, so He took her aside, and in the sweet intimacies of mutual love her fears and distrust have vanished like the mists of the morning before the rising sun.

But now that she has learned to know Him, she has a further experience of His love. He is not ashamed to acknowledge her publicly.

> He brought me to the banqueting house,
>> and his intention toward me was love. (2:4)

The house of wine is now as appropriate as the King's chambers were. Fearlessly and without shame she can sit at His side, His acknowledged spouse, the bride of His choice. Overwhelmed with His love she exclaims,

> Sustain me with raisins,
>> refresh me with apples;
>> for I am faint with love.
> O that his left hand were under my head,
>> and that his right hand embraced me! (2:5–6)

Now she finds the blessedness of belonging. No longer her own, heart-rest is her right and her enjoyment; and so the Bridegroom would have it.

I adjure you, O daughters of Jerusalem,
     by the gazelles or the wild does:
do not stir up or awaken love
     until [she] is ready! (2:7)

It is never by His will that our rest in Him is disturbed. Thus the words of the old hymn:

You may always be abiding,
If you will, at Jesus' side;
In the secret of His presence
You may every moment hide.

There is no change in His love; He is the same yesterday, today, and forever. To us He promises, "I will never leave you, never fail you, nor forsake you," and His earnest exhortation and command is "Abide in me, and I in you."

2

Communion Broken
. . . and Restored

Song of Solomon 2:8–3:5

Therefore we must pay greater attention to what we
have heard, so that we do not drift away from it.
—Hebrews 2:1

*A*t the close of the first section, we left the bride satisfied
and at rest in the arms of her Beloved, who had charged
the daughters of Jerusalem to not stir up or awaken His
love until she is ready. We might well suppose that a
union so complete, a satisfaction so full, would never be
interrupted by failure on the part of the happy bride. But
of course, the experience of most of us shows how easily
communion with Christ can be broken and how necessary are the exhortations of our Lord to those who are
indeed branches of the true Vine and cleansed by the

Word that He has spoken, to abide in Him. The failure is never on His part: "And remember, I am with you always." But the bride often forgets the exhortation addressed to her in Psalm 45:10–11:

> Hear, O daughter, consider and incline your ear;
>> forget your people and your father's house,
>> and the king will desire your beauty.
> Since he is your lord, bow to him.

In this section, the bride has drifted back from her position of blessing into a state of worldliness. Perhaps the very restfulness of her newfound joy has made her feel too secure. Perhaps she thought that so far as she was concerned there was no need for the exhortation "Little children, keep yourselves from idols." Maybe she imagined that the love of the world was so thoroughly removed from her that she could safely go back and, by a little compromise on her part, win her friends to follow her Lord too. Perhaps she scarcely thought at all: glad that she was saved and free; forgetting that the current (the course of this world) was against her, she insensibly glided, drifted back to that position out of which she was called, unaware all the time of backsliding. It is not necessary when the current is against us to turn the boat's head downstream in order to drift or for a runner in a race to turn back in order to miss the prize.

How often the enemy succeeds by one device or another in tempting the believer away from that position of entire consecration to Christ in which alone the fullness of His power and His love can be experienced. We say the *fullness* of His power and His love, for the believer may not have ceased to love his Lord.

In the passage before us, the bride still loves Him truly, though not wholly. There is still a power in His Word that is felt, though she no longer renders instant obedience to it. She does not realize that she is wronging her Lord or how real is the wall of separation between them. To her, worldliness seems but a small thing. She has not realized the solemn truth of many passages in the Word of God that speak in no uncertain terms of the folly, the danger, and the sin of friendship with the world.

Do not love the world or the things in the world. The love of the Father is not in those who love the world.

Adulterers! Do you not know that friendship with the world is enmity with God? Therefore whoever wishes to be a friend of the world becomes an enemy of God.

Do not be mismatched with unbelievers. For what partnership is there between righteousness and lawlessness? Or what fellowship is there between light and darkness? What agreement does Christ have with Beliar? Or what does a believer share with an unbeliever?

Therefore come out from them,
and be separate from them . . .
and touch nothing unclean;
then I will welcome you.
and I will be your father,
and you shall be my sons and daughters,
says the Lord Almighty.
(1 John 2:15; James 4:4; 2 Corinthians 6:14–15, 17–18)

We have to make our choice; we cannot enjoy both the world and Christ.

The bride has not learned this; she would enjoy both with no thought of their incompatibility. She observes with joy the approach of the Bridegroom:

The voice of my beloved!
Look, he comes, leaping upon the mountains,
bounding over the hills.
My beloved is like a gazelle or a young stag.
Look, there he stands behind our wall, gazing in at the
windows, looking through the lattice. (2:8–9)

The heart of the bride leaps upon hearing the voice of her Beloved as He comes in search of her. He has crossed the mountains. He draws near to her. He stands behind the wall. He even looks in at the windows. With tender and touching words He woos her to come to Him. He utters no reproach, and His loving entreaties sink deep into her consciousness.

> My beloved speaks and says to me:
> "Arise, my love, my fair one,
>   and come away;
> for now the winter is past,
>   the rain is over and gone.
> The flowers appear on the earth;
>   the time of singing has come,
> and the voice of the turtledove
>   is heard in our land.
> The fig tree puts forth its figs,
>   and the vines are in blossom;
>   they give forth fragrance.
> Arise, my love, my fair one,
>   and come away" (2:10–13).

All nature is responsive to the return of the summer; will you, my bride, be irresponsive to my love?

> "Arise, my love, my fair one,
>   and come away."

Can such pleading be in vain? Yes, it can. And it was!

In yet more touching words the Bridegroom continues:

> O my dove, in the clefts of the rock,

> in the covert of the cliff,
> let me see your face,
> > let me hear your voice;
> for your voice is sweet,
> > and your face is lovely. (2:14)

What a wonderful thought that God should desire fellowship with us and that He whose love once made Him the Man of Sorrows may now be made the Man of Joys by the loving devotion of human hearts!

But strong as His love is and His desire for His bride, He can come no further. Where she is now He can never come. But surely she will go to Him. Doesn't He have a claim upon her? She feels and enjoys His love; will she let His desire count for nothing? Note that it is not the bride who is longing in vain for her Lord but the Bridegroom who is seeking her. Can it be that He seeks her in vain?

> Catch us the foxes,
> > the little foxes,
> that ruin the vineyards—
> > for our vineyards are in blossom. (2:15)

He continues. The intruders may be small, but the mischief done is great. A little spray of blossom so tiny as to be scarcely perceived is easily spoiled, but thereby the fruitfulness of a whole branch may be forever de-

40

stroyed. And how numerous the little foxes are! A little compromise with the world; disobedience to the still, small voice in little things; little indulgences of the flesh to the neglect of duty; small neglects, doing evil in little things that good may come; and the beauty and fruitfulness of the vine are sacrificed!

We have a sad illustration of the deceitfulness of sin in the response of the bride. Instead of bounding forth to meet Him, she first comforts her own heart by the remembrance of His faithfulness and of her union with Him:

> My beloved is mine and I am his;
>> he pastures his flock among the lilies. (2:16)

My position is one of security. I have no need to be concerned about it. He is mine and I am His, and nothing can alter that relationship. I can find Him at any time; He feeds His flock among the lilies. While the sun of prosperity shines upon me, I may safely enjoy myself here without Him. Should trial and darkness come, He will surely not fail me.

> Until the day breathes
>> and the shadows flee,
> turn, my beloved, be like a gazelle
>> or a young stag on the cleft mountains. (2:17)

Careless of His desire, she lightly dismisses Him with the thought, *A little later I may enjoy His love*, and the grieved Bridegroom departs.

Poor, foolish bride! She will soon find that the things that once satisfied her can satisfy no longer and that it is easier to turn a deaf ear to His tender call than to recall or find her absent Lord.

The day became cool and the shadows did flee away, but He did not return. Then in the solemn night she discovered her mistake. It was dark and she was alone. Retiring to rest, she still hoped for His return—the lesson that worldliness is an absolute bar to full communion still unlearned.

> Upon my bed at night
>> I sought him whom my soul loves;
> I sought him, but found him not;
>> I called him, but he gave no answer. (3:1)

She waits and becomes weary. His absence becomes insupportable:

> "I will rise now and go about the city,
>> in the streets and in the squares;
> I will seek him whom my soul loves."
>> I sought him, but found him not. (3:2)

How different her position from what it might have

been! Instead of seeking Him alone, desolate, and in the dark, she might have gone out with Him in the sunshine, leaning upon His arm. She might have exchanged the partial view of her Beloved through the lattice, when she could no longer say "nothing between," for the joy of His embrace and His public confession of her as His chosen bride!

> The sentinels found me,
>> as they went about in the city.
> "Have you seen him whom my soul loves?"
> Scarcely had I passed them,
>> when I found him whom my soul loves.
> (3:3–4a)

She had already obeyed His command, "Arise . . . and come away." Fearless of reproach, she sought Him in the dark; and when she began to confess her Lord, she found Him and was restored to His favor:

> I held him, and would not let him go
>> until I brought him into my mother's house,
>> and into the chamber of her that conceived
>>> me. (3:4b)

The new Jerusalem above is our true home. There it is that full communion is enjoyed, not in worldly ways or self-willed indulgence.

Communion fully restored, the section closes as did

the first, with the loving charge of the Bridegroom that none should disturb His bride:

> I adjure you, O daughters of Jerusalem,
>> by the gazelles or the wild does:
> do not stir up or awaken love
>> until [she] is ready! (3:5)

May we all while living down here—in the world but not of it—find our home in the heavenly places to which we have been raised and in which we are seated together with Christ. Sent into the world to witness for our Master, may we ever be strangers here, ready to confess Him the true object of our soul's devotion.

> How lovely is your dwelling place,
>> O LORD of hosts!
> My soul longs, indeed it faints
>> for the courts of the LORD;
> my heart and my flesh sing for joy
>> to the living God.
> Happy are those who live in your house,
>> ever singing your praise.
> For a day in your courts is better
>> than a thousand elsewhere.
> I would rather be a doorkeeper
>> in the house of my God
> than live in the tents of wickedness.
> For the LORD God is a sun and shield;

he bestows favor and honor.
No good thing does the LORD withhold
    from those who walk uprightly.
O LORD of hosts,
    happy is everyone who trusts in you.
(Psalm 84:1–2, 4, 10–12)

3

The Joy of Unbroken Communion

Song of Solomon 3:6–5:1

O Jesus, King most wonderful,
Thou Conqueror renowned.
Thou sweetness most ineffable,
in whom all joys are found!
Thee, Jesus, may our voices bless;
Thee may we love alone;
and ever in our lives express
the image of Thine own.

In sections 1 and 2, we were mainly occupied with the words and experiences of the bride. In this section, our attention is first called to the Bridegroom; from Him we hear of the bride as the object of His love and the delight of His heart. The daughters of Jerusalem are the first speakers.

> What is that coming up from the wilderness,
>> like a column of smoke,
>
> perfumed with myrrh and frankincense,
>> with all the fragrant powders of the merchant? (3:6)

They themselves give the reply:

> King Solomon made himself a palanquin
>> from the wood of Lebanon.
>
> He made its posts of silver,
>> its back of gold, its seat of purple;
>
> its interior was inlaid with love. (3:9–10)
>
> Look, it is the litter of Solomon!
>
> Around it are sixty mighty men
>> of the mighty men of Israel,
>
> all equipped with swords
>> and expert in war,
>
> each with his sword at his thigh
>> because of alarms by night. (3:7–8)

In these verses, the bride is not mentioned; she is eclipsed in the grandeur and the state of her royal Bridegroom; nevertheless, she is both enjoying and sharing it. The very air is perfumed by the smoke of the incense that ascends pillarlike to the clouds, and all that safeguards the position of the Bridegroom himself and shows forth

His dignity safeguards also the accompanying bride, the sharer of His glory. The carriage in which they sit is built of fragrant cedar from Lebanon, and the finest of gold and silver have been lavished in its construction. The fragrant wood typifies the beauty of sanctified humanity, while the gold reminds us of the divine glory of our Lord and the silver of the purity and preciousness of His redeemed and peerless church. The imperial purple with which it is lined tells us of the Gentiles—the daughter of Tyre has been there with her gift—while the love-gifts of the daughters of Jerusalem accord with the prophecy "Even the rich among the people shall entreat your favor."

These are the things that attract the attention of the daughters of Jerusalem, but the bride is occupied with the King himself, and she exclaims,

> Come out.
> Look, O daughters of Zion,
>   at King Solomon,
> at the crown with which his mother crowned him
>   on the day of his wedding,
>   on the day of the gladness of his heart. (3:11)

The crowned King is everything to her, and she would have Him be everything to the daughters of Zion. She dwells with delight on the gladness of His heart on the day of His wedding, for now she is not occupied with Him for her *own* sake but rejoices in His joy at finding in her *His* satisfaction. Do we sufficiently cultivate this unselfish desire to be all for Jesus and to do all for His pleasure? Or are we conscious that we principally go to Him for our own sake or at best for the sake of our friends and family? How much of prayer begins and ends with the creature, forgetful of the privilege of giving joy to the Creator! Yet it is only when He sees in our unselfish love and devotion to Him the reflection of His own that His heart can feel full satisfaction and pour itself forth in precious utterances of love such as those we find in the following words:

> How beautiful you are, my love,
>> how very beautiful!
>
> Your eyes are doves
>> behind your veil.
>
> Your hair is like a flock of goats,
>> moving down the slopes of Gilead.
>
> Your teeth are like a flock of shorn ewes
>> that have come up from the washing,
>
> all of which bear twins,
>> and not one among them is bereaved.
>
> Your lips are like a crimson thread,
>> and your mouth is lovely.
>
> Your cheeks are like halves of a pomegranate
>> behind your veil. (4:1–3)

We have already found the explanation of the fairness of the bride in her reflecting like a mirror the beauty of the Bridegroom. Well may He with satisfaction describe her beauty while she is thus occupied with Him! The lips that speak only of Him are like a crimson thread; the mouth or speech that has no word of self or for self is lovely in His sight.

How sweet His words of appreciation and commendation were to the bride we can well imagine, but her joy was too deep for expression. She was silent in her love. She would not *now* think of sending Him away until the day was cool and the shadows were gone.

Still less does the Bridegroom think of finding His joy apart from His bride. He says,

> Until the day breathes
> and the shadows flee,
> I will hasten to the mountain of myrrh
> and the hill of frankincense. (4:6)

Separation never comes because of any withdrawing on His part. He is always ready for communion with a prepared heart, and in this happy communion the bride becomes even fairer and more like her Lord. She is being progressively changed into His image from one degree of glory to another through the wondrous working of the Holy Spirit, until the Bridegroom can declare:

You are altogether beautiful, my love;
there is no flaw in you. (4:7)

And now she is *fit for service*, and to it the Bridegroom woos her. She will not now misrepresent Him:

Come with me from Lebanon, my bride;
come with me from Lebanon.
Depart from the peak of Amana,
from the peak of Senir and Hermon,
from the dens of lions,
from the mountains of leopards. (4:8)

"Come with me." It is always so. When our Savior says, "Go therefore and make disciples of all nations," He precedes it with "All authority in heaven and on earth has been given to me" and follows it with "Remember, I am with you always" (Matthew 28:18–19). Or when He calls His bride to come as He does here, it is still "with me," and it is *in connection with this loving invitation* that for the first time He changes the word my "love" for the still more endearing term, my "bride."

What are lions' dens when the Lion of the tribe of Judah is with us, or mountains of leopards when He is at our side! "I will fear no evil, for you are with me." On the other hand, it is while His own is facing dangers and toiling with Him in service that He says,

You have ravished my heart, my sister, my bride,

> you have ravished my heart
>> with a glance of your eyes,
>> with one jewel of your necklace. (4:9)

Isn't it wonderful how the heart of our Beloved can be stolen by the love of one who accepts His invitation to go forth with Him to seek and to rescue the perishing? The marginal reading of the *Revised Version* says, "Thou hast given me courage." If the Bridegroom's heart may be encouraged by the fidelity and loving companionship of his bride, it is not surprising that we may cheer and encourage one another in our mutual service. The apostle Paul had a steep mountain of difficulty to climb when he was being led as a captive to Rome, not knowing the things that awaited him there, but when the brethren met him at the Appii Forum, he thanked God and took courage. May we also strengthen one another's hands in God!

The Bridegroom cheers the tedious ascents and steep pathways of danger with sweet communications of His love:

> How sweet is your love, my sister, my bride!
>> how much better is your love than wine,
>> and the fragrance of your oils than any spice!
> Your lips distill nectar, my bride;
>> honey and milk are under your tongue;

the scent of your garments is like the scent of
Lebanon.
A garden locked is my sister, my bride,
a garden locked, a fountain sealed.
Your channel is an orchard of pomegranates
with all choicest fruits,
henna with nard,
nard and saffron, calamus and cinnamon,
with all trees of frankincense,
myrrh and aloes,
with all chief spices—
a garden fountain, a well of living water,
and flowing streams from Lebanon. (4:10–15)

Engaged with the Bridegroom in seeking to rescue the perishing, the utterances of her lips are to Him as honey and the honeycomb, and metaphor upon metaphor is employed to express His satisfaction and joy. She is a garden full of precious fruits and delightful perfumes, but a garden enclosed; the fruit she bears may bring blessing to many, but the garden is for himself alone; she is a fountain, but a spring shut up, a fountain sealed. And yet again she is a fountain of gardens, a well of living waters and flowing streams from Lebanon: She carries fertility and imparts refreshment wherever she goes; and yet it is all of Him and for Him.

The bride now speaks for the second time in this section. As in her first utterance, she speaks only of Him; self is found in neither.

> Awake, O north wind,
>> and come, O south wind!
> Blow upon my garden
>> that its fragrance may be wafted abroad.
> Let my beloved come to his garden,
>> and eat its choicest fruits. (4:16)

She is ready for any experience: the north wind and the south may blow upon her garden, if only the spices thereof may flow out to regale her Lord by their fragrance. He has called her His garden, a paradise of pomegranates and precious fruits; let Him come into it and eat His precious fruits.

To this the Bridegroom replies,

> I come to my garden, my sister, my bride;
> I gather my myrrh with my spice,
> I eat my honeycomb with my honey,
> I drink my wine with my milk. (5:1a)

Now when she calls, He answers at once. When she is only for her Lord, He assures her that He finds all His satisfaction in her.

The section closes with the bride's invitation to His friends and hers, as well as to himself:

Eat, friends, drink,
  and be drunk with love. (5:1b)

The consecration of all to our Master, far from lessening our power to impart, increases both our power and our joy in service. The five loaves and two fish of the disciples, first given up to and blessed by the Lord, were abundant supply for the needy multitudes, and increased while being distributed until twelve baskets were filled with the leftover fragments after everyone was satisfied.

We see in this beautiful section a picture of unbroken communion and its delightful results. May our lives ever correspond! First, one with the King, then speaking of Him; the joy of communion leading to fellowship in service, to being all for Jesus, ready for any experience that will fit for further service; surrendering all to Him, and willing to minister in all for Him. There is no room for love of the world here, for union with Christ has filled the heart. It has been sealed and is kept for the Master's use.

Jesus, my life is Thine!
And evermore shall be
hidden in Thee.
For nothing can untwine
Thy life from mine.

4

Communion Broken Again . . . and Restored

Song of Solomon 5:2–6:10

———

*T*his section commences with an address of the bride to the daughters of Jerusalem, in which she narrates her recent sad experience and entreats their help. The presence and comfort of her Bridegroom are again lost to her, not by relapse into worldliness but by slothful self-indulgence.

We are not told of the steps that led to her failure, of how self again found a place in her heart. Perhaps spiritual pride in the achievements that grace enabled her to accomplish was the cause. Or a cherished satisfaction in the *blessing* she had received—instead of in the Blesser himself—may have led to the separation. She seems to be largely unconscious of her declension. Self-occupied and self-contented, she scarcely notices His absence. She is resting, resting alone—never asking where He has gone or how He is employed. And more than this, the door of her chamber is not only closed but barred—an evidence that His return is neither eagerly desired nor expected.

Yet her heart is not far from Him. There is a music in His voice that awakens echoes in her soul such as no other voice could have stirred. She is still "a garden shut up, a fountain sealed" so far as the world is concerned. The snare this time is the more dangerous and insidious because it is quite unsuspected. Let us look at her narrative:

> I slept, but my heart was awake.
> Listen! my beloved is knocking.
> "Open to me, my sister, my love,
>   my dove, my perfect one;
> for my head is wet with dew,
>   my locks with the drops of the night" (5:2).

How often the position of the Bridegroom is that of a knocking suitor outside as in His epistle to the Laodicean church: "Listen! I am standing at the door knocking; if you hear my voice and open the door, I will come in to you and eat with you, and you with me" (Revelation 3: 20). It is sad that He should be outside a closed door—

that He should need to knock—but still more sad that He should knock in vain at the door of any heart that has become His own. In this case, it is not the *position* of the bride that is wrong. If it were, His word as before would be, "Arise . . . and come away"; whereas now His word is "Open to me, my sister, my love." It was her *condition* of self-satisfaction and love of ease that closed the door.

Very touching are His words, "Open to me, my sister" (He is the firstborn among many brethren), "my love" (the object of my heart's devotion), "my dove" (one who has been endued with many of the gifts and graces of the Holy Spirit), "my perfect one" (washed, renewed, and cleansed for me); and He urges her to open by reference to His own condition: "for my head is wet with dew, my locks with the drops of the night."

Why is it that His head is wet with dew? Because His heart is a shepherd-heart. There are those whom the Father has given to Him who are wandering on the dark mountains of sin. How many have never heard the Shepherd's voice? And many who were once in the fold have wandered away—far from its safe shelter. The heart that can never forget, the love that can never fail, *must* seek the wandering sheep until the lost one has been found: "My Father works, and I work." And will she, who so recently was at His side, who joyfully braved the dens of lions and the mountains of leopards, will she leave Him to seek alone the wandering and the lost?

> "Open to me, my sister, my love,
>> my dove, my perfect one;
> for my head is wet with dew,
>> my locks with the drops of the night" (5:2b).

We do not know a more touching entreaty in the Word of God, and sad indeed is the reply of the bride:

> I had put off my garment;
>> how could I put it on again?
> I had bathed my feet;
>> how could I soil them? (5:3)

Sadly, it is possible to take delight in conferences and conventions, to feast on all the good things that we enjoy as Christians, and yet be unprepared to go out from them to self-denying efforts to rescue the lost. It is easy to delight in the rest of faith and forget about fighting the good fight of faith; to dwell upon the cleansing and the purity effected by faith but to have little thought for souls struggling in the mire of sin. If we can put off our coat when He would have us keep it on, if we can wash our feet while He is wandering alone upon the mountains, is there not a sad lack of fellowship with our Lord?

Having no response from the bride, the Bridegroom seeks to enter through the door:

> My beloved thrust his hand into the opening,
>> and my inmost being yearned for him. (5:4)

But remember, the door was not only latched, it was barred; and His effort to secure an entrance was in vain.

> I arose to open to my beloved,
>> and my hands dripped with myrrh,
> my fingers with liquid myrrh,
>> upon the handles of the bolt.
> I opened to my beloved,
>> but my beloved had turned and was gone.
> My soul failed me when he spoke. (5:5–6a)

When all too late the bride arose, she seemed to be more concerned about anointing herself with liquid myrrh than about welcoming her waiting Lord, more occupied with her own graces than with His desire. No words of welcome were uttered, though her heart sank within her, and the grieved One had withdrawn himself before she was ready to receive Him. Again, as in section 3, she had to go forth alone to seek her Lord, and this time her experiences were much more painful than before.

> I sought him, but did not find him;
>> I called him, but he gave no answer.
> Making their rounds in the city
>> the sentinels found me;

they beat me, they wounded me,
　they took away my mantle,
　　those sentinels of the walls. (5:6b–7)

Her first relapse had been one of inexperience. If a second relapse came about inadvertently, she should at least have been ready and prompt when summoned to obey. It is not a small thing to fall into the habit of being late in obedience, even in the case of a believer. In the case of the unbeliever, the final issue of disobedience is inexpressibly awful:

Give heed to my reproof;
I will pour out my thoughts to you;
　I will make my words known to you.
Because I have called and you refused,
　have stretched out my hand and no one
　　heeded. . . .
I also will laugh at your calamity;
　I will mock when panic strikes you. . . .
Then they will call to me, but I will not answer;
　they will seek me diligently,
　　but will not find me.
(Proverbs 1:23–24, 26, 28)

The backsliding of the bride, though painful, was not final, for it was followed by true repentance. She went forth into the darkness and sought Him. She called, but

He did not respond, and the watchmen finding her, both beat and bruised her. They appear to have appreciated the gravity of her error more than she did. Believers may be blinded to their own inconsistencies; others, however, note them, and the closer one has been to the Lord the more certain will any distance be visited with reproach.

Wounded, dishonored, unsuccessful in her search, and almost in despair, the bride turns to the daughters of Jerusalem and, recounting the story of her sorrows, adjures *them* to tell her Beloved that she is not unfaithful or unmindful of Him.

> I adjure you, O daughters of Jerusalem,
>> if you find my beloved,
> tell him this:
>> I am faint with love. (5:8)

The reply of the daughters of Jerusalem shows very clearly that the sorrow-stricken bride, wandering in the dark, is not recognized as the bride of the King, though her personal beauty does not escape their notice.

> What is your beloved more than another beloved,
>> O fairest among women?
> What is your beloved more than another beloved,
>> that you thus adjure us? (5:9)

This question, implying that her Beloved was no better than any other, stirs her soul to its deepest depths, and forgetting herself, she pours out from the fullness of her heart a soul-swelling description of the glory and beauty of her Lord:

My beloved is all radiant and ruddy,
    distinguished among ten thousand. (5:10)

(See also vv. 11–15.)

His speech is most sweet,
    and he is altogether desirable.
This is my beloved and this is my friend,
    O daughters of Jerusalem. (5:16)

It is interesting to compare the bride's description of the Bridegroom with the descriptions of the Ancient of Days in Daniel 7:9–10 and of our risen Lord in Revelation 1:13–16.

In Daniel 7, we see the Ancient of Days seated on the throne of judgment. His clothing was white as snow, and the hair of His head like pure wool. His throne was fiery flames, and its wheels were burning fire. A stream of fire issued and flowed out from His presence. One like a human being coming with the clouds of heaven was presented before Him and was given dominion and glory and kinship. His dominion is an everlasting dominion that shall not pass away. In Revelation 1, we see the Son of Man himself dressed in a long robe, and His head and His hair are white as white wool, as white as snow; but the bride sees her Bridegroom in all the vigor of youth, with locks "wavy and black as a raven." The eyes of the risen Savior are described as "a flame of fire," but His bride sees them "like doves beside springs of water." In Revelation, "His voice is like the sound of rushing waters . . . and out of his mouth comes a sharp, double-edged sword." To the bride, "His lips are lilies, distilling liquid myrrh" and "His speech is most sweet." The face of the risen Savior is "like the sun shining with full force," and the effect of the vision on John—"When I saw him, I fell at his feet as though dead"—was not unlike the effect of the vision given to Saul as he neared Damascus. But to His bride, "His appearance is like Lebanon, choice as the cedars." The Lion of the tribe of Judah is to His own bride the King of love, and, with full heart and beaming face, she so recounts His beauties that the daughters of Jerusalem are seized with strong desire to seek Him with her, that they also may behold His beauty.

> Where has your beloved gone,
>   O fairest among women?
> Which way has your beloved turned,
>   that we may seek him with you? (6:1)

The bride replies,

My beloved has gone down to his garden,
>   to the beds of spices,
> to pasture his flock in the gardens,
>   and to gather lilies.
> I am my beloved's and my beloved is mine;
>   he pastures his flock among the lilies. (6:2–3)

Forlorn and desolate as she might appear, she still knows herself as the object of His affection, and claims Him as her own. This expression, "I am my beloved's and my beloved is mine," is similar to that found in the second section, "My beloved is mine and I am his," yet with a noteworthy difference. Then her first thought of Christ was of her claim upon Him; His claim upon her was secondary. Now she thinks first of His claim and only afterward mentions her own. We see a still further development of grace in 7:10, where the bride, losing sight of her claim altogether, says,

> I am my beloved's,
>   and his desire is for me.

No sooner has she acknowledged herself as His rightful possession (6:3)—a claim she had practically repudiated when she kept Him barred out—than her Bridegroom himself appears. With no upbraiding word, but in tenderest love, He tells her how beautiful she is in His eyes and speaks her praise to the daughters of Jerusalem.

To her, He says,

> You are beautiful as Tirzah, my love,
>> comely as Jerusalem,
>> terrible as an army with banners.
> Turn away your eyes from me,
>> for they overwhelm me! (6:4–5a)
> (See also vv. 5b–7.)

Then, turning to the daughters of Jerusalem, He exclaims,

> There are sixty queens and eighty concubines,
>> and maidens without number.
> My dove, my perfect one, is the only one,
>> the darling of her mother,
>> flawless to her that bore her.
> The maidens saw her and called her happy;
>> the queens and concubines also, and they
>>> praised her.
> "Who is this that looks forth like the dawn,
>> fair as the moon, bright as the sun,
>> terrible as an army with banners?" (6:8–10)

And so this section closes with communion fully restored, the bride reinstated and openly acknowledged by the Bridegroom as His own peerless companion and friend. The painful experience through which the bride has passed has been filled with lasting good, and we have no further indication of interrupted communion but only joy and fruitfulness.

5

The Fruits of a Recognized Union

Song of Solomon 6:11–8:4

*I*n sections 2 and 4, we found the communion of the bride broken—first, by backsliding into worldliness, and then through slothful ease and self-satisfaction. This section, like the third, is one of unbroken communion. It is opened by the words of the bride:

> I went down to the nut orchard,
>> to look at the blossoms of the valley,
> to see whether the vines had budded,
>> whether the pomegranates were in bloom.
> Before I was aware, my fancy set me
>> in a chariot beside my prince. (6:11–12)

As in the opening of section 3, the bride, in unbroken communion with her Lord, is present though unmentioned, until she makes her presence evident by her address to the daughters of Zion. So also in this section, the presence of the King is unnoted until He addresses His bride. But she is one with her Lord as she engages in His service! His promise, "Remember, I am with you always," is a constant fulfillment to her. He no longer has to woo her to arise and come away, to tell her that His "head is wet with dew," His "locks with the drops of the night," or to urge her if she love Him to feed His sheep and care for His lambs. She is herself His garden, and she does not forget to tend it, nor keep the vineyards of others while her own is neglected. *With* Him as well as *for* Him, she goes to the nut orchard.

So thorough is the union between the bride and the Bridegroom that many commentators have had difficulty deciding which is the speaker here. It doesn't really matter, for, as we have said, both are present and of one mind, yet I suggest that the words are the bride's, as she is the one addressed by the daughters of Jerusalem and the one who speaks to them in reply.

The bride and Bridegroom appear to have been discovered by their willing people while thus engaged in the happy fellowship of fruitful service, and the bride, before she is aware of it, finds herself seated among the chariots of her people—*her* people as well as *His*.

The daughters of Jerusalem would call her back:

Return, return, O Shulammite!
Return, return, that we may look upon you. (6:13)

There is no question now as to who she is or why her Beloved is more than another beloved. He is recognized as King Solomon, and to her is given the same name, only in its feminine form, *Shulammite*.

Some have seen in the words "Return, return" an indication of the rapture of the church, and explain some parts of the subsequent context that appear inconsistent with this view as resumptive rather than progressive. As interesting as this thought is, and the fact that it would explain the absence of *reference* to the King in the preceding verses, I am not inclined to accept it, but rather look on the whole song as progressive and its last words as being equivalent to the closing words of Revelation: "Surely I am coming soon. Amen. Come, Lord Jesus!" I do not, therefore, look upon the departure of the bride from her garden as being other than temporary.

The bride replies to the daughters of Jerusalem, "Why should you look upon the Shulammite?" Or, as in the King James Version, "What will ye see in the Shulamite?"

In the presence of the King, she cannot conceive why any attention should be paid to *her*. As Moses was unconscious that his face shone with a divine glory as he came down from the mount, so it is with the bride. But we may learn this very important lesson, that many who do not see the beauty of the Lord will not fail to admire His reflected beauty in His bride. The eager look of the daughters of Jerusalem surprised the bride, and she compares their look to that of someone looking upon "a dance before two armies" [the dance of two companies of Israel's fairest daughters] instead of upon one who has no claim for attention, save that she is the chosen, though unworthy, bride of the glorious King.

The daughters of Jerusalem have no difficulty in replying to her wonderment. Recognizing her as one of royal birth—"O queenly maiden!"—as well as of queenly dignity, they describe in true and Oriental language the tenfold beauties of her person. From her feet to her head they see only beauty and perfection. What a contrast to her state by nature! Before, she was from the sole of her foot even to her head covered with wounds and bruises and festering sores; now her feet are shod with the preparation of the gospel of peace, and the very hair of her head proclaims her a Nazarite indeed—the King himself is held captive by her tresses.

But her Beloved responds to her unaffected question, "Why should you look upon the Shulammite?"

How fair and pleasant you are,
O loved one, delectable maiden! (7:6)

He sees in her the beauties and the fruitfulness of the tall and upright palm, of the graceful and clinging vine, of the fragrant and evergreen citron. Grace has made her like the palm tree, the emblem of both uprightness and fruitfulness. The fruit of the date-palm is more valued than bread by the Oriental traveler, so great is its sustaining power. The fruit-bearing powers of the tree do not pass away; as age increases the fruit becomes more perfect as well as more abundant.

> The righteous flourish like the palm tree,
>> and grow like a cedar in Lebanon.
> They are planted in the house of the LORD;
>> they flourish in the courts of our God.
> In old age they still produce fruit;
>>> they are always green and full of sap. (Psalm 92:
>> 12–14)

Why are the righteous upright and flourishing?

> Showing that the LORD is upright;
>> he is my rock, and there is no unrighteousness
>>> in him. (Psalm 92:15)

One with our Lord, it is ours to *show forth* His graces and virtues, to reflect His beauty, to be His faithful witnesses.

The palm is an emblem of victory. It raises its beautiful crown toward the heavens, fearless of the heat of the sun or of the hot wind from the desert. Because of its beauty, it was one of Solomon's ornaments, as it is to be of Ezekiel's temple. When our Savior was received at Jerusalem as the King of Israel, the people took branches of the palm tree to greet Him; and in that glorious day of His wedding feast, a great multitude that no one can count, from every nation, from all tribes and peoples and languages, shall stand before the throne and before the Lamb, robed in white, with palm branches in their hands, and cry out in a loud voice, "Salvation belongs to our God who is seated on the throne, and to the Lamb!" (See Revelation 7:9–10.)

But if the bride resembles the palm, she also resembles the vine. She needs the tending of the Husbandman, and she well repays His kind attentions. Abiding in Christ, the true source of fruitfulness, she brings forth clusters of grapes, luscious and refreshing as well as sustaining, like the fruit of the palm—luscious and refreshing to himself, the owner of the vineyard, as well as to the weary, thirsty world in which He has placed it.

The vine has its own implied lessons: it needs and seeks support; the sharp knife of the Pruner often cuts away unsparingly its tender garlands and mars its appearance, while increasing its fruitfulness. It has been beautifully written:

The living Vine, Christ chose it for Himself:

74

God gave to man for use and sustenance
Corn, wine, and oil, and each of these is good:
And Christ is Bread of life and Light of life.
But yet, He did not choose the summer corn,
That shoots up straight and free in one quick growth,
And has its day, is done, and springs no more;
Nor yet the olive, all whose boughs are spread
In the soft air, and never lose a leaf,
Flowering and fruitful in perpetual peace;
But only this, for Him and His are one—
That everlasting, ever-quickening Vine,
That gives the heat and passion of the world,
Through its own life-blood, still renewed and shed.
The Vine from every living limb bleeds wine;
Is it the poorer for that spirit shed?
The drunkard and the wanton drink thereof;
Are they the richer for that gift's excess?
Measure thy life by loss instead of gain;
Not by the wine drunk, but the wine poured forth;
For love's strength standeth in love's sacrifice;
And whoso suffers most, hath most to give.

Yet one more metaphor is used by the Bridegroom:
"The scent of your breath [is] like apples [citrons]." In the
first section the bride exclaims,

As an apple tree among the trees of the wood,
    so is my beloved among young men.

With great delight I sat in his shadow,
  and his fruit was sweet to my taste. (2:3)

Here we find the outcome of that communion. The citrons she ate perfumed her breath, imparting to her their delicious fragrance. The Bridegroom concludes his description:

and your kisses like the best wine
  that goes down smoothly. (7:9a)

The bride interjects,

  gliding over lips and teeth. (7:9b)

How wondrous the grace that has made the bride of Christ to be all this to her Beloved! Upright as the palm, victorious, and evermore fruitful as she grows heavenward; gentle and tender as the Vine, self-effacing and self-sacrificing, not merely bearing fruit in spite of adversity, but bearing her richest fruits through it; feasting on her Beloved, as she rests beneath His shade, and thereby partaking of His fragrance—what has grace not done for her! And what must be her joy in finding, ever more fully, the satisfaction of the glorious Bridegroom in the lowly wild flower He has made His bride, and beautified with His own graces and virtues! She gladly exclaims,

I am my beloved's,
  and his desire is for me. (7:10)

Now it is none of self or for self, but all of Thee and for Thee. And if such be the sweet fruits of going down to the nut orchard and caring for His garden with Him, she will need no constraining to continue in this blessed service.

Come, my beloved,
let us go forth into the fields,
and lodge in the villages. (7:11)

She is not ashamed of her lowly origin, for she fears no shame. Perfect love has cast out fear. The royal state of the King, with its pomp and grandeur, may one day be enjoyed: now it is more sweet with Him at her side to make the garden fruitful; to give to Him all manner of precious fruits, new and old, which she has laid up in store for Him; and best of all, to satisfy Him with her own love. Not only is she contented with this fellowship of service but she wishes that there were no honors or duties to claim His attention and for the moment lessen the joy of His presence.

O that you were like a brother to me,
who nursed at my mother's breast!
If I met you outside, I would kiss you,
and no one would despise me. (8:1)

She wishes that she could care for Him and claim His

whole attention as a sister might care for a brother. She is deeply conscious that He has richly endowed her and that she is nothing compared to Him. But instead of proudly dwelling upon what she has done through Him, she wishes that it were possible for her to be the giver and He the receiver. This is far removed from the grudging thoughts some have that must grate upon the heart of our Lord: "I do not think that God requires this of me" or "Must I give up that, if I am to be a Christian?" True devotion asks to be allowed to give, and will count as loss all that may not be given up for the Lord's sake. "I count all things but loss, for the excellency of the knowledge of Christ Jesus my Lord," said Paul. Longing desire to be more to Him does not, however, blind the bride to the consciousness that she needs His guidance and that He is her true and only Instructor.

> I would lead you and bring you
>> into the house of my mother,
>>> and into the chamber of the one who bore me.
> I would give you spiced wine to drink,
>> the juice of my pomegranates. (8:2)

I would give Thee my best, and yet would myself seek all my rest and satisfaction in Thee.

> O that his left hand were under my head,
>> and that his right hand embraced me! (8:3)

And thus the section closes. There is nothing sweeter to the Bridegroom or to the bride than this hallowed and unhindered communion. And again He adjures the daughters of Jerusalem, in slightly different form:

I adjure you, O daughters of Jerusalem,
> do not stir up or awaken love until [she] is ready!
> (8:4)

Hallowed communion, indeed! May we ever enjoy it, and, abiding in Christ, we shall sing, in the familiar words of the well-known hymn,

Both Thine arms are clasped around me,
And my head is on Thy breast;
And my weary soul hath found Thee
Such a perfect, perfect rest!
Blessed Jesus,
Now I know that I am blest.

6

Unrestrained Communion

Song of Solomon 8:5–14

We have now reached the closing section of this book, The Song of Songs, which, as we have seen, is a poem describing the life of a believer on earth. Beginning in section 1 (1:2–2:7) with the unsatisfied longings of the bride—longings that can only be met by her unreserved surrender to the Bridegroom of her soul—we find that when the surrender is made, instead of the cross she had so much feared, she finds a King, the King of Love, who both satisfies her deepest longings and finds His own satisfaction in her.

The second section (2:8–3:5) shows some failure on her part. She is lured back into the world, and soon finds that her Beloved cannot follow her there. Then, with full purpose of heart, going out to seek Him and confess His name, her search is successful and communion restored.

The third section (3:6–5:1) tells of an unbroken communion. Abiding in Christ, she shares His security and His glory. She draws the attention of the daughters of Jerusalem, however, from these outward things to her King himself. And while she is thus occupied with Him, and would have others so occupied, she finds that her royal Bridegroom is delighting in her and inviting her to fellowship of service, fearless of dens of lions and mountains of leopards.

The fourth section (5:2–6:10), however, shows again failure on the bride's part; not as before through worldliness, but rather through spiritual pride and sloth. Now restoration is much more difficult, but again, when she goes forth diligently to seek her Lord and to confess Him so as to lead others to long to find Him with her, He reveals himself to her and communion is restored to be interrupted no more.

The fifth section (6:11–8:4) describes not only the mutual satisfaction and delight of the bride and Bridegroom in each other but also the recognition by the daughters of Jerusalem of her position and her beauty.

Now in the sixth section (8:5–14), we come to the closing scene of the book. In it, the bride is seen leaning upon her Beloved, asking Him to bind her yet more firmly to himself, and occupying herself in His vineyard until He calls her away from earthly service.

This section opens, as did the third, by an inquiry or exclamation of the daughters of Jerusalem. There they asked, "What is that coming up from the wilderness, like a column of smoke...?" but then their attention was claimed by the pomp and state of the King, not by His person or by that of His bride. Here they are attracted by the happy position of the bride in relation to her Beloved, and not by their surroundings.

> Who is that coming up from the wilderness,
>> leaning upon her beloved? (8:5a)

It is through the bride that attention is drawn to the Bridegroom; their union and communion are now open and manifest. For the last time the wilderness is mentioned; but sweetly solaced by the presence of the Bridegroom, it is not a wilderness to the bride. In all the trust of confiding love she is seen leaning upon her Beloved. He is her strength, her joy, her pride, and her prize, while she is His peculiar treasure, the object of His most tender care. All His resources of wisdom and might are hers; though journeying, she is at rest; though in the wilderness, she is satisfied while leaning upon her Beloved.

But as wonderful as the revelations of grace and love are to the heart taught by the Holy Spirit through the relationship of bride and Bridegroom, the Christ of God is more than a Bridegroom to His people. He who while on earth was able to say, "Before Abraham was, I am," here claims His bride from her very birth, not only from her present relationship to Him. Before she knew Him, He knew her, and of this He reminds her in the words:

Under the apple tree I awakened you.
There your mother was in labor with you;
    there she who bore you was in labor. (8:5b)

He takes delight in her beauty, but that is not so much the cause as the effect of His love, for He took her up when she had no attraction. The love that made her what she is, and now takes delight in her, is not a fickle love, nor need she fear its change.

Gladly does the bride recognize this truth, that she is indeed His own, and she exclaims,

Set me as a seal upon your heart,
    as a seal upon your arm;
for love is strong as death,
    passion fierce as the grave.
Its flashes are flashes of fire,
    a raging flame. (8:6)

The High Priest bore the names of the twelve tribes upon his heart, each name being engraved as a seal in the costly and imperishable stone chosen by God, each seal or stone being set in the purest gold; he likewise bore the same names upon his shoulders, indicating that both the love and the strength of the High Priest were pledged on behalf of the tribes of Israel. The bride would be thus borne by Him who is alike her Prophet, Priest, and King, for love is strong as death, and jealousy, or ardent love, retentive as the grave. Not that she doubts the constancy of her Beloved, but that she has learned, alas, the inconstancy of her own heart, and she would be bound to the heart and arm of her Beloved as with chains and settings of gold, even the emblem of deity. Thus the psalmist prayed, "Bind the sacrifice with cords, even unto the horns of the altar."

It is comparatively easy to lay the sacrifice on the altar that sanctifies the gift, but it requires divine compulsion—the cords of love—to retain it there. So here the bride would be set and fixed on the heart and on the arm of Him who is from here on to be her all in all, that she may evermore trust only in that love, be sustained only by that power.

Do we not all need to learn a lesson from this? and to pray to be kept from turning to Egypt for help, from trusting in horses and chariots, from putting confidence in princes or in the son of man rather than in the living God? How the kings of Israel, who had won great triumphs by faith, sometimes turned aside to heathen nations in their later years! The Lord keeps His people from this snare.

To the bride's description of her passion and her request to be set as a seal upon His heart, the Bridegroom replies with reassuring words:

> Many waters cannot quench love,
>> neither can floods drown it.
> If one offered for love
>> all the wealth of his house,
>> it would be utterly scorned. (8:7)

The love that grace has begotten in the heart of the bride is itself divine and persistent; many waters cannot quench it, nor the floods drown it. Suffering and pain, bereavement and loss may test its constancy, but they will not quench it. Its source is not human or natural. Like our life, it is hidden with Christ in God:

> Who will separate us from the love of Christ? Will hardship, or distress, or persecution, or famine, or nakedness, or peril, or sword? . . . No, in all these things we are more than conquerors through him who loved us. For I am convinced that neither death, nor life, nor angels, nor rulers, nor things present, nor things to come, nor powers, nor height, nor depth, nor anything else in all creation, will be able to separate us from the love of God in Christ Jesus our Lord. (Romans 8:35, 37–39)

Our love to God is secured by God's love to us. To the soul truly rescued by grace, no bribe to forsake God's love will be finally successful. "If one offered for love all the wealth of his house, it would be utterly scorned."

Freed from anxiety on her own account, the happy bride next asks guidance and fellowship in service with her Lord on behalf of those who have not yet reached her favored position.

> We have a little sister,
>   and she has no breasts.
> What shall we do for our sister,
>   on the day when she is spoken for? (8:8)

How beautifully her conscious union with the Bridegroom appears in her expression: "*We* have a little sister," not *I* have . . . ; "What shall *we* do for our sister?" She has neither private relationships nor interests; in all things she is one with Him. And we see a further development of grace in the very question. Toward the close of the last section, she recognizes the Bridegroom as her Instructor. She will not now make her own plans about her little sister and then ask His blessing in them. She will rather learn what His thoughts are and fellowship with Him in His plans.

How much anxiety and care the children of God would be spared if they learned to act in this way! Isn't it common to make the best plans that we can and to carry them out as best we can, feeling all the while a great burden of responsibility and earnestly asking the Lord to help us? Whereas if we always let *Him* be our Instructor in service, and leave the responsibility with *Him*, our strength would not be exhausted with worry and anxiety, but all would be at His disposal and would accomplish His ends.

In the little sister, as yet immature, we see the elect of God given to Christ in God's purpose but not yet brought into a saving relationship with Him. Perhaps also is seen those babes in Christ who as yet need to be fed with milk and not with meat, but who, with proper care, will in due time become dedicated believers, fit for the service of the Lord. Then they will be spoken for, that is, called into the service for which He has created them and prepared them.

The Bridegroom replies,

> If she is a wall,
>   we will build upon her a
>   battlement of silver;
> but if she is a door,
>   we will enclose her with
>   boards of cedar. (8:9)

In this reply, the Bridegroom sweetly recognizes His

oneness with His bride, in the same way as she has shown her conscious oneness with Him. As she says, "What shall *we* do for our sister?" so He replies, "*We* will build . . . *we* will enclose." He will not carry out His purposes of grace irrespective of His bride, but will work with and through her. What is done for this sister, however, will depend upon where she is in relation to the Bridegroom. If she be a wall, built upon the true foundation, strong and stable, she shall be adorned and beautified with battlements of silver. But if unstable and easily moved to and fro like a door, such treatment will be as impossible as unsuitable—she will need to be enclosed with boards of cedar, hedged in with restraints for her own protection.

The bride responds, rejoicing, "I am a wall." She knows the foundation on which she is built. There is no doubt in her case. She is conscious of having found favor in the eyes of her Beloved. Naphtali's blessing is hers: she is "satisfied with favor, and full with the blessing of the Lord."

But what is taught by the connection of this happy consciousness with the lines that follow?

Solomon had a vineyard at Baal-hamon;
  he entrusted the vineyard to keepers;
  each one was to bring for its fruit a thousand

pieces of silver.
My vineyard, my very own, is for myself;
    you, O Solomon, may have the thousand,
    and the keepers of the fruit two hundred!
(8:11–12)

I believe the connection is one of great importance, teaching us that what she *was* (by grace) was more important than what she *did*, and that she did not work in order to earn favor, but being assured of favor, gave her love free scope to show itself in service. The bride knew her relationship to her Lord and His love to her. And in her determination that He should have the thousand pieces of silver, her concern was that her vineyard should not produce less for her Solomon than His vineyard at Baal-hamon. Her vineyard was herself, and she desired for her Lord much fruit. She would see, too, that the keepers of the vineyard, those who were her companions in its culture, and who ministered in word and doctrine, were well rewarded. She would not muzzle the ox that treaded out the corn. A full tithe, even a double tithe, was to be the portion of those who kept the fruit and labored with her in the vineyard.

How long this happy service continues, and how soon it is to be terminated, we cannot tell. He who calls His servants to dwell in the gardens and cultivate them for Him—as Adam of old was placed in the Paradise of

God—alone knows the limit of that service. Sooner or later rest will come, the burden and heat of the last day will have been borne, the last conflict will be over, and the voice of the Bridegroom will be heard addressing His loved one:

> O you who dwell in the gardens,
>> my companions are listening for your voice;
>> let me hear it. (8:13)

Your service among the companions is finished. You have fought the good fight, you have finished the race, you have kept the faith. From now on there is reserved for you the crown of righteousness, and the Bridegroom himself shall be your exceeding great reward! (See 2 Timothy 4:7–8.)

Well may the bride let Him hear her voice, and, springing forth in heart to meet Him, cry,

> Make haste, my beloved,
>> and be like a gazelle
> or a young stag
>> upon the mountains of spices! (8:14)

She no longer asks Him, as in the second section,

> Turn, my beloved, be like a gazelle
>> or a young stag on the cleft mountains. (2:17b)

She has never again wished Him to turn away from

her, for there are no such mountains to those who are abiding in Christ; now there are mountains of spices. He who inhabits the praises of Israel, which rise like the incense of spices from His people's hearts, is invited by His bride to make haste, to be like a gazelle or a young stag upon the mountains of spices.

Very sweet is the presence of our Lord as by His Spirit He dwells among His people while they serve Him below. But here there are many thorns in every path, which call for watchful care, and it is fitting that we should suffer with our Lord in order that we may hereafter be glorified together. The day is coming, however, in which He will bring us up out of the earthly gardens and associations to the palace of the great King. There His people "will hunger no more, and thirst no more; the sun will not strike them, nor any scorching heat; for the Lamb at the center of the throne will guide them to springs of the water of life, and God will wipe away every tear from their eyes" (Revelation 7:16–17).

The Spirit and the bride say, "Come!" . . .
"Surely I am coming soon."
    Amen. Come, Lord Jesus!
(Revelation 22:17, 20)

Appendix

The Daughters of Jerusalem

———

*T*he question is frequently asked, "Who are represented by the daughters of Jerusalem?"

They are clearly not the bride, yet they are not far removed from her. They know where the Bridegroom makes His flock to rest at noon; they are charged by the Bridegroom not to stir up nor awaken His love when she rests, abiding in Him. They draw attention to the Bridegroom as with dignity and pomp He comes up from the wilderness. Their love-gifts adorn His chariot of state. They are appealed to by the bride for help in finding her Beloved, and, stirred by her impassioned description of His beauty, they desire to seek Him with her. They describe very fully the beauty of the bride, but on the other hand, we never find them occupied with the *person* of the Bridegroom; *He* is not all in all to them; they mind outward and earthly things.

Do they not represent those who are for the present

more concerned about the things of this world than the things of God? To advance their own interests and to secure their own comfort concerns them more than to be in all things pleasing to the Lord. They *may* form part of that great company spoken of in Revelation 7:9–17 who come out of the great tribulation, but they will not form part of the 144,000, the firstfruits unto God and to the Lamb (Revelation 14:1–5). They have forgotten the warning of our Lord in Luke 21:34–36, and hence they are not accounted worthy to escape all these things that shall come to pass, and to stand before the Son of Man. They have not, with Paul, counted "all things but loss for the excellency of the knowledge of Christ Jesus the Lord."

I must place on record the solemn conviction that not all who are called Christians, or think themselves to be such, will attain to that resurrection of which Paul speaks in Philippians 3:11, or will thus meet the Lord in the air. Unto those who by lives of consecration manifest that they are not of the world but are looking for Him, He will appear without sin unto salvation.